Harriet Mallard

**Bible Evergreens for Christmas**

Harriet Mallard

**Bible Evergreens for Christmas**

ISBN/EAN: 9783743387386

Manufactured in Europe, USA, Canada, Australia, Japa

Cover: Foto ©Lupo / pixelio.de

Manufactured and distributed by brebook publishing software
(www.brebook.com)

Harriet Mallard

**Bible Evergreens for Christmas**

# BIBLE EVERGREENS

FOR

## CHRISTMAS.

BY HARRIET MALLARD

"How excellent is thy loving-kindness, O God! therefore the children of men put their trust under the shadow of thy wings."—PSALM XXXVI: 7.

NEW YORK:

BAKER & GODWIN, PRINTERS,

PRINTING-HOUSE SQUARE.

1872.

# BIBLE EVERGREENS.

## A Saviour which is Christ the Lord.

A Saviour which is Christ the Lord!
Seraphic notes proclaim the word,
Angels of light His godhead own,
And from the high eternal Throne
Announce the long-expected One—
The great Jehovah's mighty Son,
A glorious Prince, to be adored—
A Saviour which is *Christ the Lord.*

The Son of God, to sinners given;
Glory to Him in highest Heaven;
New joys immortal now have birth,
Good will to men and peace on earth,
This natal day of holy things;
We've tidings born on heavenly wings—
Let every soul the song record
A Saviour which is Christ the Lord.

It dawned for bliss this welcome day;
He comes! the life, the truth, the way,
The great efficient sacrifice,
The one that love divine supplies,
To ransom from the power of sin,
A crown unfading he shall win
For all that choose his ways, his words;
*This Saviour, He is Christ the Lord.*

## Let there be Light.

"The spirit of God moved upon the face of the waters, and God said, Let there be light, and there was light."

Athwart the broad chaotic night
A voice is heard : let there be light ;
And darkness, with relinquished rein,
To lucid beauty yields the plain.

Let there be light ; an orb of fire—
A globe of glory—bids retire
The shades that wrapped this earthly ball
Around, as by some ebon pall.

Let there be light ; creation's bloom
Smiles out from void and sightless gloom.
Let there be light ; the lovely queen
Of eve her placid face is seen.

Let there be light ; of spirit power,
'T has come at God's appointed hour.
Let there be light ; a star appears—
'Tis Bethlehem's Star—the hope of years.

Now on the long bewildered sight
It sheddeth rays, redeeming—bright ;
It luminates the path—the way
That leadeth to eternal day.

## The Unrejected Offering.

"And the Lord had respect unto Abel, and to his offering."

Mercy, with heaving bosom, stood
There by that altar, bathed in blood,
Where first the "righteous Abel" lies—
The typifying sacrifice.

The mystic flood, the crimson stream,
It shadows forth that darling theme
Which filled her gentle beaming eye;
There, the Immortal Fountain nigh.

When love divine a "ransom found,"
By which the sinner, lost and bound,
Should be redeemed, and saved, and shriven,
And find Eternal Life in Heaven.

There list'ning, while on hallowed air,
Faith pours the early trustful prayer,
She sees the savoury incense rise,
Accepted far above the skies.

We read it in symbolic lines
Of what that Counsel High designs,
Of the triumphant glorious reign
Of One from "The Foundation slain."

# A Precious Promise.

### "I will not leave you comfortless."

I will not leave you comfortless !
   Oh, precious heavenly word.
I will not leave you comfortless,
   Thus saith our gracious Lord.

'Twas on the last sad evening
   In which he was betrayed,
To the beloved disciples—
   Some doubting—all afraid :

"Let not your heart be troubled,"
   For you I will prepare,
And yet know the way that leadeth
   To the heavenly mansions fair.

It is for this I'm going
   To prepare a place for you,
And I'll come and will receive you—
   My glory you shall view.

"I will not leave you comfortless ;"
   Ask, ever in my name ;
I am the Mediator,
   I will present your claim,

To my Father ever merciful,
   He ne'er will thee deny ;
Ask in the name of Jesus
   And mercy shall be nigh.

I will not leave you joyless—
I'll send him to abide—
The Holy Ghost, the Comforter,
With richest gifts supplied.

Now, if you love the Father,
And Jesus Christ the Son, ·
And God the Holy Spirit,
*Thy heaven is now begun.*

Keep faithful my commandment;
Keep, ever keep my word,
Then he that dwelleth with you
Shall be your guide and guard.

Keep this, my new commandment,
And love each other too,
Then, the all-sufficient Comforter
Shall always be with you.

## The Resurrection and the Life.

"Jesus said, I am the resurrection and the life, he that believeth in me,
though he were dead, yet shall he live."

Jesus wept—
Though strong to save,
Then called the sleeper
From the grave ;
With godlike voice,
Divine and loud,
He claimed of death
The youthful prey ;

His mighty bars
He bursts away,
Lo ! Lazarus wrapt
In burial shroud.

The scoffer, now
With dread surprise;
Sees at His call the dead arise
And leave the dark abode;
And many there
The word believed,
And Christ, the Nazarene received,
And owned the Son of God !

## With Christ is Paradise.

" And he said unto Jesus, Lord remember me when thou comest into thy kingdom." "And Jesus said unto him, Verily I say unto thee, to-day shalt thou be with me in Paradise.

The conflict now with justice, stern,
    And death, its close is near;
The malefactor's fainting heart—
    'Tis perishing in fear :
The heavens above his guilty head
    Frown everlasting night,
While memory's page of sin—of crime—
    Is black before his sight.
And earth with callous, tearless eye,
    Upon the sword, hath smiled,
That mortal hand thus holds severe
    To pierce her fallen child.

Sacred compassion standeth near,
 And claimeth to preside,
That for the sufferer's penitence,
 A space she may provide.
Love, everlasting love divine,
 'Twas thine alone—the power—
Contrition timely to bestow
 At the expiring hour.
Grace, sovereign, saving, heavenly grace.
 Was pleased then to attest
Its own supreme efficiency
 To make the vilest blest.
The hopeless, dying one his need
 'Tis given him deep to feel,
And faith to cry—to look to Him
 Who can his pardon seal.
Jesus, the mighty Son of God,
 Responsive to his prayer,
He saith, To-day in Paradise,
 Thou shalt be with me there.

## The Many Mansions.

"In my Father's house are many mansions. If it were not so I would have
told you."

Saviour, yes, thou wouldst have told us
 If thy Father's house had place
Not for us—the earth-worn, weary,
 Saved by thy triumphant grace.

Faith descrieth now the mansions
  Where thy ransomed soon shall rest—
Bowers of holy light and beauty
  Which thy loving hand hath dressed—

Everlasting habitations
  Ready waiting there to greet
All that in the heavenly kingdom
  Ask through Christ, a share—a seat.

Glorified, divine Redeemer,
  Hope hath triumphed o'er the gloom
Once that tried our fainting spirit,
  Resting on the grave—the tomb.

Son of God! that upper temple,
  Luminated now by Thee—
We believe its bliss eternal
  Thou hast willed that we shall see.

## Free Indeed.

"If the Son shall make you free, then shall you be free indeed."

Son of God, the price to free—
Faith beholds it—paid by thee;
What eternal wisdom willed,
Jesus, thou hast now fulfilled.

Thou from the foundation slain,
Thou in Zion chosen, lain—
Heaven's appointed corner stone,
Here as our Emanuel known.

Thou hast made us free, indeed;
Thou dost with the Father plead—
All-sufficient sacrifice—
Slain with thee, with thee we rise.

Wake we from the sleep of sin
Strong in thee, the crown to win
Of life—and by thy saving power
Find we now Thy name a tower.

## God is Love.

God, the mighty, great, and wise,
 Omnipresent Lord of power,
Reigning, ruling earth and skies—
 Life sustaining every hour,
Giver of creation's breath,
 Center of the world above,
He that holds the keys of death
 Is the God of deathless love.

Holy justice, stern, severe,
 Claiming every title still;
When He came the sad to cheer—
 Great Redeemer, to fulfill
All the pleasure of the Lord,
 Price he offered that may prove
That which claimed the long award—
 That may witness "God is Love."

God of mercy, truth, and peace,
 Come and sanctify this heart;

Bid these gloomy fears to cease—
  Give assurance of a part
With the blessed Prince of Life;
  Come, thou ever-kindly dove;
Thou canst end all doubt and strife—
  Thou canst witness "God is Love."

King of Kings, before whose throne
  Heavenly hosts their crowns they cast;
He who is the Lord alone—
  Great, Eternal, First and Last;
Holy Judge of quick and dead,
  At whose voice the pillars move
Of the universe He spread,
  Calls His name the "God of Love."

---

## Salvation of the Lord.

### "Salvation belongeth unto the Lord."

Poor doubting, fearing, trembling soul,
  Benighted where the blast
Is threatening loud thy shivering bark,
  Come, and thy anchor cast,
Where waves of wrath—of death and sin
  Obey the mighty voice
Of Jesus, who controls the storm—
  Make now this port your choice.

When moored within this haven fair
  All clouds shall disappear;
"The Christ," the Sun of Righteousness,
  Thy fainting soul will cheer;

The tempest-toss'd on sorrow's sea
  Shall find, for every ill,
An all-sufficient, perfect cure,
  When bending to His will.

Before the highest throne of heaven
  They chant this blissful song;
The saved by grace, the justified,
  The happy, ransomed throng—
To Christ the Lord, our righteousness,
  Belongs eternal praise;
He only hath salvation,
  This ancient one of days.

## Our Advocate.

"We have an advocate with the Father, Jesus Christ the righteous, who ever
liveth to make intercession for us."

Sorrowing one, dismiss thy fear,
Let the Word thy spirit cheer;
Jesus, Advocate, in love
Pleads thy cause in courts above;
Christ, the Mediator, there
Counts thy tears—he hears thy prayer;
Great High Priest, within the vail
Offering that which shall prevail,
And acceptance find for thee,
And secure thy pardon free;
Holy incense, all divine,
Richer far than rubic mine—

Sacred drops—with sovereign power
They demand a plenteous shower—
Shower of all-sufficient grace
Sprinkling for the fallen race.

All that turn and look shall live,
Life and hope are his to give ;
An Advocate at God's right hand
Doth thy pardon full demand ;
He the hopeless debt for thee
Paid—and now he saith, be free—
Free to share my pardoning love
And the mansions built above ;
Now, behold the open door ;
Enter ye, and fear no more.

## He Loved them to the end.

" Having loved his own that were in the world, he loved them to the end."

Jesus, the holy Son of God,
　　The hopeless sinner's friend,
While dwelling with humanity
　　He loved—loved to the end.

When that dark hour was nearing
　　When crimson drops should stain
The sod of sad Gethsemane,
　　That witnessed to his pain,
His more than mortal agony
　　When He the cup received

And drank, that so the captive
　Of death should be reprieved;
While envy, wrath and mockery
　Their voices loudly blend,
He loved His own—this Saviour—
　He loved them to the end.

Come, now, ye sorrowing, doubting,
　And at his cross low bend;
He'll succour, save and pardon,
　And love thee to the end.

Have shafts of cruel hatred
　Thy spirit grieved and riven—
No ear of human sympathy
　To thee been lent or given?
Then to this Mediator
　Thy deepest woes reveal—
Thy care, thy grief, infirmity,
　He liveth now to feel.

The clouds that frown and threaten
　He will in mercy rend;
Come, prayerfully, and trust him
　That loveth to the end.

## The Beauty of Holiness.

" Worship the Lord in the beauty of holiness."

Worship the Lord
　With holy contrition;
Bow low at his feet
　In perfect submission;

Come, bring to his altar
The pure sacrifice—
The heart that is humble
He freely supplies.

With graces and beauties,
And heavenly delight
That ravish the soul
And the spirit invite
Away to the mansions,
The blissful abode
Prepared for the people—
The children of God.

O! worship the Lord
In beauty, in truth—
The strength of the aged,
The guide of the youth;
The ever-blest Father
And Son glorify,
And the Holy Spirit
That bringeth so nigh.

The perfect salvation,
A cure for our fear—
The word that enlightens
Our darkness so drear;
The glorious Trinity
Worship and adore
In the beauty of holiness
Now and evermore.

## My Strength and My Redeemer.

"Let the words of my mouth, and the meditations of my heart, be acceptable in thy sight, O Lord, my strength and my Redeemer."

Now from every earthly refuge,
    Saviour, I would turn to Thee;
Thou my strength and my Redeemer,
    Deign my darkened soul to free—
Break the yoke of heavy bondage—
    Unbelief—and bid retire
All but min'string spirits holy,
    Angels, such as shall inspire
Heaven accepted meditations;
    Let my words but speak thy praise,
And let thy indwelling spirit
    Give me songs of love to raise;
Indite for me my petitions
    When before thy throne I come;
Guide me ever by thy presence,
    Bring me gently, safely home.

## Wait on the Lord.

"Wait on the Lord, be of good courage, and he shall strengthen thy heart."

Christian, from thy fear and trembling,
    Rise, and to that altar fly,
Where the heart, when brought an offering,
    "Saving health" it findeth nigh;
Grace divine, and all-sufficient,
    There shall bid thy soul be strong

When, at Mercy's footstool waiting,
    Hope and joy shall be thy song;
Wait, and thou shalt find thy helmet,
    That which shall not fade or fail,
And entire thy mail—thy armor—
    That which shall thy need avail.

---

## Heavenly Care.

"The needy shall not always be forgotten; the expectation of the poor shall
not perish forever."

All thy hopes they shall not perish,
    Child of poverty and care,
Heaven thy fainting heart will cherish,
    Let thy trust be centred there.

Ever mindful of the sparrow;
    Sooner such will God forget,
Than his poor, when want and sorrow
    May their pilgrim path beset.

Now thy unbelief dismissing,
    Bid the morrow's empty board
Wait, nor ask to-day the service
    Which the dawn may see restored.

Expectations—fondest, dearest—
    Are they at the point to die?
Clouds surcharged that now thou fearest
    Mercy bid, may pass thee by.

## Compassed by Heavenly Favor.

" For thou, Lord, wilt bless the righteous; with favor wilt thou compass him
as with a shield."

With the heavenly favor shielded,
  Servants of the Lord of life,
Though the storms of danger thicken,
  Pass they safe the bounds of strife.

Mercy there the portal keepeth,
  Where the righteous seeketh rest,
Pity there, she never sleepeth
  When the justful are oppressed.

Love's own fount that faileth never,
  Springing holy ever free,
Shall their need supply forever,
  Here and through eternity.

---

## I will cry unto God.

" I will cry unto God most high, unto God that performeth all things for me."

Let me find a timely refuge,
  Lord of love, beneath the shade,
Shelt'ring wings that shall not weary
  When the tempest doth pervade.

Even now, the storm it rageth,
  Winds most pitiless they blow,
Earth refuseth her defences,
  Grief my spirit bendeth low.

Hope that strove and o'er the sadness
    Held a flickering lamp of light,
Fainted while we saw it smothered,
    Not to glad again the sight.

Let me fly, O God, to hide me
    Where the strife shall pass me by,
At thy word there shall be stillness,
    Let me, Abba Father, cry.

Send thou, mighty One from heaven,
    Mercy; envoys too, of power;
Let thy truth be found an helmet
    For thy saved, this needful hour.

---

## The Children's Blessing.

"Suffer little children to come unto me."

Oh favored children thus caress'd,
In Jesus' arms received and bless'd;
The heirs of heaven accepted made,
His sacred hand in love was laid
In tenderest mercy on your head,
With dews of grace divinely shed.

Forbid them not to come to Me,
They are my lambs, and they shall see
The pastures of my glorious rest.
Come, little children, come be blest,
For them I have a high abode—
The heavenly kingdom of my God.

Of such the throng now shelter'd there,
I make the little ones my care ;
O bring them on the arms of faith,
In love the Holy Saviour saith,
I will transplant them 'bove the skies,
To bloom for aye in Paradise.

The darling flowers—the plants of earth—
Shall know a new immortal birth ;
The fairest here, they bloom to die,
But life—new Life—I will supply.
O, bring the children to the Lord,
He will fulfill his gracious word.

## Glad News.

"Zion heard, and was glad."

Glad news, glad news for Zion !
    Is floating on the breeze,
For many a heathen nation
    The heavenly light now sees.

The isles that deck the ocean,
    The gospel banner hail;
They cheer with true devotion,
    And welcome every sail

That wafts the story-thrilling
    Of our redeeming God,
And blessed feet most willing
    To press the mountain's sod,

That come with spirits burning
  To publish pard'ning peace,
And ardent bosoms yearning
  To bid their idols cease.

Lo! on the distant hill-tops,
' Where mystic altars blaze,
A new and crystal fountain
  Its healing power displays.

Rejoice, rejoice, Oh Zion now!
  See Mercy's chariot rolls;
O! help and early pay the vow,
  Its resting place the poles.

---

## The Day Star.

Light, celestial orbs eclipsing,
  Day-star, in our hearts arise;
Spirit of the true adoption,
  Come and bear us to the skies.

On the wings of faith transport us
  And permit a heavenly view
Of the Tree of Life there blooming,
  Ever verdant, ever new.

Glad we hail the blessed tidings
  Of this glorious Eastern Star;
Star of hope, of life eternal,
  Radient still in lands afar.

Blessed star, thou still art guiding
　Ever with thy quenchless light;
From the gloomy vales of darkness
　Thou dispellest death and night.

Where the reign of sin and terror
　Held an undisputed sway,
There the brightness of thy rising
　Rends the thickest films away.

Now the dawn of life immortal
　Greets the waiting heathen eye;
God the Father, Son, and Spirit,
　Brings the full salvation nigh.

## Distrust not the Lord.
### "Why are ye so fearful?"

Why are ye so fearful?
　Sad victim of care;
The Lord, the great shepherd,
　His pastures are fair;
Besprinkled with manna,
　A daily supply—
Oh, why are ye fearful?
　His mercy is nigh.

Though filled with the tempest,
　Be drenched by the storm;
He'll smooth the rough waters,
　His word will perform;

He's reigning in glory,
    He sleepeth no more,
He's bread for the hungry
    And care for the poor.

To heirs of salvation
    His tokens of love
Are angels attendant
    Sent forth from above ;
Oh, trust in his mercy,
    Obeying his will ;
The storms that assail thee,
    He'll bid them " Be still."

## The Love of Christ;

" Who shall separate us from the love of Christ,"

Oh, triumph in redeeming love,
    Ye children, heirs of grace,
You're called, and justified, and saved,
    In Heaven you have a place.

Ah, who is he that may condemn,
    'Tis Christ that died for thee ;
All things are yours, and freely given,
    The Kingdom you shall see ;

Nay, more, the conqueror's crown, through him,
    Jesus, the Saviour, Lord,
That fills the mediatorial throne
    Shall be your blest reward.

Shall persecution's dread array,
    With all her boasted power,
Combined with famine, want and pain—
    Dark tribulation's hour,

Or sin, or death, or aught presume,
    Of all these present things
To drive the saved, the ransomed soul
    From His kind, shelt'ring wings.

Oh! love divine, through Him, the Christ,
    Thou'lt bring us safely home,
Persuaded by the Spirit's breath
    We'll fear no things to come.

## Our High Priest.

"Casting all your care upon him, for he careth for you,"

Casting all your care upon Him,
    On the word of Jesus lean ;
Humbly trusting in his mercy,
    Soon his hand it shall be seen.

For His sympathizing bosom,
    "Great High Priest," is touched for thee ;
Though within the vail now entered,
    He thy grief and want will see.

Once he press'd an earthly pillow,
    Once he wore a thorny crown ;
And a storm of fierce temptations
    Sought to bend his spirit down.

Christ that knew of constant sorrows;
　Made acquainted oft with grief,
Lives to feel for thy affliction;
　He will send thee sweet relief.

Cast thy care, believe and trust Him,
　Watch to know and do His will,
You shall find that daily manna
　Lacketh not thy board to fill.

## The Lord thy Shade.

"The Lord is thy shade upon thy right hand."

The Lord that built the heavens·
　And earth's foundation laid,
He is thy life, thy portion,
　Thy refuge, strength, and shade;

Thy helper and redeemer
　From sorrow, sin and wrong;
Thy shepherd, friend and keeper,
　Oh, bring a grateful song.

Come ye before his presence
　·With off'ring of his choice—
The heart, the willing incense,
　Responsive to his voice.

The Lord, he will preserve thee,
　Will set thy spirit free
From death and sin's dark bondage
　Christ hath atoned for thee.

Come, now, by faith relying
 Upon his holy word;
Leave all for this inheritance,
 The kingdom of your Lord.

He is a tower, a shadow,
 A rock, a resting place;
He'll shed on thee abundantly
 His free, abounding grace.

---

## The Servants of Righteousness.

"Being then made free from sin, ye became the servants of righteousness,"

Dost thou find the fetters broke;
 Bonds of sin their strong control;
Welcome ye the Master's yoke?
 Answer—hopeful, trusting soul;
Dost thou find thy willing heart
 Leaping to obey the call
Of righteousness, though bid to part
 With hidden idols, one and all?
Then the Son hath made you free,
 And we hail thee free, indeed;
You by grace the land shall see
 Where the ransomed flock shall feed,
Led by Him, the Lamb, the Lord,
 Jesus, now the glorified,
'Tis by his unfailing word
 That with Him ye shall abide.

## Redemption.

"The Lord redeemeth the soul of his servants, and none of them that trust in
him shall be desolate."

Servant of the living God,
    If thy spirit, weary, faints,
Christ, the mighty to redeem,
    Shields the weakest of his saints.

Desolation's cheerless shade
    Shall not cross thy pilgrim way;
Clouds that gather thick and fast
    Shall not hide the heavenly ray
Of the Sun of Righteousness,
    Beaming from the fount of light;
Sorrow, with her mantle cold,
    May not screen it from thy sight.

Love divine, it faileth not,
    Though thy flesh, thy heart expire;
Soon thy soul among the just
    Shall possess a raptured lyre;
Clad in robe prepared of love,
    Shall have entered into rest,
Where the loudest notes ecstatic
    Are by ransomed ones expressed.

## The Fullness of Christ.

" For it pleased the Father that in him should all fullness dwell."

Fullness of eternal wisdom,
    Fullness of abounding grace,
Fullness of complete redemption,
    Fullness, too, of lasting peace.

Dwell in Him, the blessed image
  Of the great Invisible;
Son of the eternal Father,
  Transcript of his holy will.

Fullness of life-giving power,
  Strength of heaven for all the weak,
Armor for the holy warfare,
  For the helpless, faint and weak.

Weak in faith and "poor in spirit,"
  Servants of this gracious Lord,
Now the voice of saving mercy
  Calls you to the heavenly board ;

Bids you to the feast of fullness,
  Ocean of that water pure,
Love's unmeasured, free salvation,
  Sin's immortal, perfect cure.

Riches of the full assurance
  Of the hope of life and heaven ;
Anchor for the trembling vessel
  From his fullness, ready given.

Knowledge, truth, and love, and mercy,
  Gifts, a free, exhaustless store
Dwell in Him, the Mediator,
  To dispense to all the poor.

## Heaven-born Charity.

"Let all your things be done with charity."

Let this queen of Christian graces,
　　Charity ; her hand supplied
With her golden, sacred scepter,
　　O'er thy walks, thy deeds, preside.

When the shiv'ring, sorrowing, knocketh—
　　Hungry at thy gate—thy door,
Let her spirit guide thee—teach thee
　　Not to bid them call no more.

Let her, when thy brother's burden
　　Presseth sore, of grief, of care,
Then sustain thy heart, thy shoulder,
　　Joyfully the weight to share.

Let her voice, of accent holy,
　　Unforbidden then be heard,
If to whelm the weak, the erring,
　　Stern reproach may be preferred.

Charity, her mantle heavenly,
　　Shall be found to pardon—hide
Sins that else to pride were deadly,
　　Christ, the robe he did provide.

# The Lord is my Shepherd.

The great Omnipresent,
  Omnipotent One,
That settled the mountains
  And fashioned the sun ;

That spread out the heavens,
  And named all the stars,
And set for the ocean
  Its bounds and its bars.

This Lord is my Shepherd,
  No want shall I know ;
A faithful, kind shepherd,
  All grace to bestow.

He is the Jehovah,
  Jehovah alone ;
I am, is the name
  By which he'll be known.

The Immortal Invisible,
  God only wise,
In sacred compassion
  He doth not despise.

Though highly exalted
  Above all the praise
That highest archangel
  Or seraphim raise ;

From the height of his glory,
　For to condescend,
To say he's my Shepherd,
　My Father, my Friend.


Yes, he is a shepherd,
　A shepherd by choice,
He said that his people
　Would all know his voice.


By name he would call them,
　And safely would lead ;
Come, follow this shepherd,—
　You never shall need.


Haste, haste to the Rock
　That was smitten for thee ;
The Rock of all Ages,
　The fountain is free.


Then come to the well-spring,
　And thirst not again ;
The shepherd will heal
　All thy sickness and pain.


Drink, drink of this water,
　And eat of this bread ;
'Tis heavenly provision,
　The table is spread.

The draught, it is healing,
  Life giving, divine ;
This proffered salvation,
  Ye doubting, is thine.

Fly, then, to the refuge,
  Be sheltered, be led—
The oil of Heaven's gladness
  Shall rest on thy head.

He leadeth in pastures
  Where evergreens grow,
And the still and deep waters,
  They cease not to flow.

You there shall recline
  In the shade of the tree ;
The shepherd's kind bosom
  Thy pillow shall be.

The tree by the side
  Of the pure, crystal river
That springs from the throne
  Of the almighty giver.

There's life in the fruit
  Which its full branches yield,
And with its broad leaves
  Shall the nations be healed.

The Lord, the Redeemer
Will surely receive—
He named the condition,
'Tis only "believe."

## Clouds Dissolving.

" Clouds and darkness are around about him, righteousness and judgment are
the habitations of his throne."

Dark, dark indeed the shades that fill
The way He bids me go;
I look for light to do His will;
I ask His truth to know.

Thick clouds portentious gather near,
And all but cast a vail
Before the eye of faith, and fear,
It would my trust assail.

Ah! unbelief, begone—I've found
His word—'tis written fair,
Though clouds and darkness, they surround,
The Lord is reigning there.

Righteous and true he shall be known;
His mercy shall appear;
" The habitation of His throne"
Is holy judgment clear.

He will preserve my waiting soul;
  He is exalted high;
His power and love are told in song
  By saints above the sky.

What heavenly light divine is sown
  For all in heart made pure;
I will rejoice in Thee alone,
  Thou blessed refuge sure.

## Purity of the Word.

"Thy word is very pure."

Thy word is very pure,
Established ever sure,
Forever to endure;
  We glorify thy name.
Thy word of truth, of power,
It cheers the darkest hour,
Though storms around may lower
  Thy word is still the same.

Thy blessed word most holy,
To all the meek and lowly
A glorious treasure truly,
  The gift, the book divine;
The volume richly stored
With words of Christ, the Lord,
By humble hearts adored—
  I call this treasure mine.

This word beyond compare
Forever may I share,
And may its truths prepare
  My soul for that abode;
Where righteousness and peace abound,
Pleasures forevermore are found,
And the redeemed the Lamb surround,
  And praise my Father, God.

## Peace, be Still.

I'm tempest tossed, on troubled waters;
  Saviour, if it be Thy will,
Touch these angry, raging billows,
  Say, in mercy, "Peace, be still."

None but Thee, O gracious Master!
  Can the tide of ills control;
Speak, and winds and waves shall own thee,
  And the surges backward roll.

Overwhelmed with grief and anguish,
  Sinketh fast this shiv'ring bark;
Hopes, they only bloom to vanish;
  Gath'ring clouds grow dark, more dark.

Let me see Thee near approaching,
  With thy peace my spirit fill;
Help, and sanctify, and save me;
  Bid these earthly cares "Be still."

## Consider the Ravens.

Consider the ravens ;
  Remember the sparrow ;
'Twill strengthen thy faith,
  And wisdom ye'll borrow :
Go learn of the insect,
  The meanest in dust,
In God, thy kind Father
  To anchor thy trust !

The raven, the sparrow,
  And all he supplies;
Every wing of light beauty
  That cleaveth the skies ;
To them neither treasure
  Or garner is given ;
Their share and their portion,
  They seek it of Heaven.

Then fear not, though
  Poverty's vale be thy lot.
Of price above sparrows
  Thou'lt ne'er be forgot;
The hand that creation
  So fully supplies,
To children choice favors
  It never denies.

## The Established Throne.

"The Lord's throne is in heaven."

God of my trust, I know thy throne
　Is high—in highest heaven,
Where songs, triumphant songs are known
　By ransomed souls forgiven.

Thy throne of mercy, gracious Lord,
　Is builded on the ground;
Established, like thy holy word
　Where life alone is found.

O Thou most holy, just, and wise,
　Permit my heart to share
The worship of the upper skies,
　To hold communion there.

Give me, O Father heavenly, kind,
　This pledge of heavenly things;
A will entire to thee resigned,
　Proof that thy spirit brings.

The earnest of indwelling grace,
　Thy presence and thy love;
The smile of my Redeemer's face,
　And bear me safe above.

Give day by day renewing power,
　And sanctify for Thee;
My soul entire for coming hour,
　That I that throne may see.

## Joy in Sorrow.

"I will be glad, and rejoice in thee."

O thou most high and holy God,
    I will rejoice in thee,
Though suff'ring now thy chast'ning rod,
    Thou'rt gracious still to me.

Thy truth and mercy shall endure
    Forever—evermore;
All earthly ills thy love can cure—
    Oh! blest eternal store.

Yes, I will glory in the Lord,
    Will be exceeding glad;
And joyful in thy heavenly word,
    Though sorrowing, sick, and sad.

The Lord will be a refuge sure
    For every child of care;
Turn now from every earthly lure,
    And life and favor share.

Go you of every form of grief,
    Approach the Saviour's feet;
Forsake your sinful unbelief,
    And mercy shall thee greet.

Her gifts are promises of peace—
    Of Heaven—immortal rest;
Jesus will bid thy anguish cease—
    Make thee supremely blest.

## Ministering Spirits.

'Tis written in thy holy word,
    In living lines—I read it plain ;
That heirs of thy salvation, Lord,
    Angelic ministers obtain.

In mercy sent—in heavenly love,
    To hold their watch around our rest,
And point us to the land above—
    How rich ! of such a guide possessed.

And have I then a guardian sent ?
    Then will I yield no more to doubt ;
I know a hand unseen was lent
    To lead from threatening dangers out.

O thou my guardian angel fair !
    Thy wing untiring grant to wave ;
Forsake me not, but safely bear,
    Away beyond the grave.

––––––

## The Covenant of Grace.

"He will ever be mindful of his covenant."

His everlasting covenant
    Of mercy, truth, and grace ;
Of peace, and life, and blessedness,
    With all the ransomed race—
Shall never be forgotten,
    But present with the Lord,
Who ever will be mindful
    Of his most holy word.

His promises of power,
  To all who ask his care ;
A never failing helper,
  And bread a daily share;
He never will forget thee—
  Thy God the word hath spoke :
His own eternal covenant,
  It never can be broke.

## Hope and Trust.

" For in thee, O Lord, do I hope."

My hope, O Lord, is anchored,
  All sure, within the vail ;
I trust thy precious promises
  Though dangers thick assail.

The waves of fierce temptation
  Besiege my trembling soul ;
But, Lord, thou wilt control them—
  Wilt bid them backward roll.

I know, O blessed Jesus,
  Thou'lt suffer but the share
That with thy grace sustaining
  I may triumphant bear.

O thou that knew temptation
  In all its varied power—
I crave thy kind assistance
  In this portentous hour.

O give me now the vict'ry,
    Be pleased to set me free;
Thy name shall have the glory,
    Thou holy One in Three.

## Quickening Grace.

"Quicken me after thy loving kindness."

O God, I ask thy quick'ning grace,
    In its renewing power;
Thy blessed promises I trace,
    But clouds around me lower;
Come, Holy Spirit, shed thy light—
    My faith is weak—I need—
I ask thy help; my prayer indite,
    Blest Saviour, intercede.

My heart is dark, and hard, and cold,
    Beset by doubts and fear;
Come, heavenly Dove, thy wing now fold
    Around my soul to cheer;
Thy loving kindness never fails,
    But, oh! this unbelief
My hope, my trust, my faith assails,
    Dear Saviour, send relief.

According to thy holy word
    So loving, heavenly, kind;
Come, sanctify my spirit, Lord,
    And help me now to find
In thee the refuge of my soul,
    A shelter from the storm;
The waves of unbelief that roll,
    And fears of every form.

## Waiting on the Lord.

"Though I walk in the midst of trouble, thou wilt revive me."

Though walking now where grief and tears
  My fearful steps surround;
And where no earthly comfort cheers
  The hopeless, barren ground;
Where troubles, like an angry storm,
  Unbidden, round me rise,
And thick'ning mists of fear transform
  My fainting hope—that dies;—
I know, O thou my heavenly friend—
  My Father—gracious, kind,
Thou wilt in mercy deign to send
  Some angel hand to bind
This spirit, that was doomed to break
  When sorrow's power was shed,
Unsparing, for thy name's dear sake
  On this poor, aching head;
Thy word shall bid each cloud remove—
  E'en now, through the disguise,
I see a token of thy love
  That yields my soul supplies;
Sweet mem'ries of thy faithful hand
  Come round me while I weep;
Ranged as a true, unyielding band
  Of sentinels, to keep
Their watch, there by the gloomy way
  Where impious unbelief

Would claim the sceptre, and display
Her banner, dyed with grief;
Thou wilt my languid faith inspire;
With joy my cup wilt fill;
Revive and tune my saddened lyre
Accordant with thy will.

## Healing Mercy.

*"He hath heard my voice, and my supplication."*

The Lord my prayer hath heard,
Hàth lent his gracious ear;
In honor of his name, his word,
I now record it here.

'Twas when o'erwhelmed with fear,
And sinking near the grave,
He came, the gracious Helper near,
In pity came to save.

My supplicating voice
Sought not His ear in vain;
In life I now rejoice,
Although to die were gain.

To die in Him, who died—
It were the dawn of day;
He hath death's power defied,
The vict'ry borne away.

The tomb his servants share
Is sacred, hallowed ground;
All that his image bear
By angels shall be found.

Be gather'd with that band—
  The ransomed that surround
The throne in that blest land
  Where joy and peace abound.

Down by the swelling surge
  Of Jordan's darksome tide—
Just on the trembling verge,
  My journey lay beside.

Long by the lonely stream
  That laves this barren shore,
My watchful spirit caught a beam
  On seraph pinions bore;

A ray of that bless'd light
  That gilds the blissful plain;
It did my soul invite
  Away from sin and pain.

It was my choice to stay,
  Though heavenly gain to go;
My loved ones by the way,
  Still on my heart, I know

By heavenly hand were laid—
  They begg'd me tarry still;
I sought His gracious aid—
  I ask'd to know his will.

It was his will to spare;
  I bless his healing hand;
His goodness now I see,
  Here in this living land.

## Mercy our Trust.

"I have trusted in thy mercy."

I have trusted in thy mercy,
   I have gloried in thy grace ;
Shall this trust be unavailing—
   Shall I seek in vain thy face.

Long, not long wilt thou forget me,
   Thou in mercy wilt appear
To dispel these storms thick gath'ring,
   Thou the darkest skies canst clear.

I have trusted in thy mercy,
   Found thy name a sure defense ;
Ever present to defend me ;
   Unbelief thou'lt banish hence !

I believe, and I will trust thee—
   Help, O help my unbelief ;
Known but unto thee, O Father,
   Each mysterious source of grief.

All-sufficient, gracious helper,
   Speak, and end the causeless strife ;
Present help in time of trouble—
   Thou the way, the truth, the life.

Early called to love and praise thee,
   And to find thy promise sure ;
I shall see thy hand revealed,
   Covenant mercy shall endure.

## Rejoice Evermore.

Rejoice, and evermore rejoice,
If you have made the better choice;
Glory in free grace, free grace,
Heaven shall be your dwelling place.

Evermore rejoice in love,
You "Our Father's" care shall prove;
Joy, and bless the favor'd day
That he turned thy feet away

From the paths of death and sin,
Bade thee seek, and saw thee win
Heaven's immortal, priceless gem,
An everlasting diadem.

More pure than all of earthly mold,
Than diamond's sheen, or finest gold,
The "Hidden Pearl;" 'tis free to all
That meekly for the treasure call.

Rejoice, the days are on the wing;
Soon with sainted choirs you'll sing:
In Father, Son, and Holy Ghost,
Joy and rejoice, and ever boast.

## Seeking Jesus.

"I know ye seek Jesus."

Fear not, you're seeking Jesus,
   The Saviour crucified;
I know you're seeking, sorrowing,
   The loving Lamb who died.

He lives again—he's risen;
   Behold, they laid him here!
I know you're seeking Jesus—
   You may dismiss your fear.

Go, quick, and tell your brethren
   He's risen from the dead:
Still seek and follow Jesus,
   The Christ—the living Head.

Behold the open sepulchre,
   Their watch the angels keep,
And all who sleep in Jesus
   Will find it precious sleep.

Now death has lost the vict'ry,
   The grave has lost its gloom;
Oh, seek and know the Victor,
   He'll bring thee from the tomb.

# The Strength of Zion.

"I will rejoice in thy salvation."

Oh! thou mighty God of Jacob—
  Strength of Zion—if thy will,
Hear us in our day of trouble,
  Our petitions now fulfill.

From thy sanctuary send us
  Thy refreshing, cheering grace;
In the name of Christ, our offering,
  These our prayers to thee we raise.

We no other trust desire,
  Than remembrance of thy power;
From thy holy heaven assist us,
  Let this be thy favor'd hour.

We'll rejoice in thy salvation,
  We will glory in thy word;
In thy name our banners raising,
  Shout thy praise, victorious Lord.

---

# All-sufficient Grace.

"My grace is sufficient for thee."

Grace, all-sufficient, heavenly grace—
  And is this promise mine?
Is it for all that seek thy face,
  Blest Jesus, thus to find

A never failing, gracious store ?
A heavenly treasure filled !
Blessings descending evermore,
Profusely round distilled.

Oh, highly favor'd, sacred hour,
That fixed my happy choice;
That witness'd thy redeeming power,
In which I now rejoice ;
All glory to thy precious name,
Thanks to thy pard'ning love,
Thanks to the Holy Spirit's flame
That came the word to prove.

There's all-sufficient, mighty grace,
For every time of need,
In Christ, the safe abiding place—
Oh heavenly, glorious meed !
From storms of danger, death, and strife,
Ye win the soul away ;
From scenes with gath'ring ills most rife,
To hopes of perfect day.

## Divine Teaching.

" O God, thou hast taught me from my youth."

Father in heaven, thy gracious hand
Hath led me all the way ;
In childhood's hour—in youth's frail morn,
Thou wast my hope, my stay.

Taught by thy word, thy spirit's voice,
  I learned thy name to fear;
To trust thy blessed promises,
  And found a helper near.

When by thy faithful, chast'ning rod,
  My heart was well subdued,
Thy reconciling love alone
  Hath all my soul renewed.

When clouds were gath'ring thick, to pour
  The storm to overwhelm
The trembling bark—a whisper spake,
  "Thy pilot's at the helm!"

Fear not, he walks upon the wave;
  He'll bid its fury cease;
He came—allayed the threat'ning surge;
  Commanded—there was peace.

---

## Quench not the Spirit.

"Quench not the spirit."

Oh! quench not the spirit,
  The spirit to thee,
Like the dove, ever gentle,
  To light or to flee—

Is seeking to win thee,
  Permit the kind guest,
Now welcome his visits—
  Allow him to rest.

Most fondly he's hovering,
　　Oh, bid him good cheer;
He'll guide thee, and guard thee,
　　Protect thee from fear.

His visits are heavenly,
　　He comes to explain
The word of the Father,
　　And Son that was slain.

If fearful, if faithless,
　　In danger to stray,
With kindness he'll lead thee,
　　And point thee the way.

And level the mountains,
　　Or storms that arise;
And fill all thy soul
　　With grateful surprise.

Quench, quench not the spirit,
　　O may he abide—
This heavenly, blest comforter,
　　Jesus supplied.

He said he would send him,
　　And he should reveal,
And on the Atonement
　　Would set his own seal.

His earnest, mysterious,
The seal of the Lord,
The faithful, true witness,
Confirms the record—

Of God, ever faithful,
Who finished—begun—
The perfect redemption
Wrought through the blest Son.

## The Charge of Angels.

"For he shall give his angels charge over thee, to keep thee in all thy ways."

What, oh, what, shall ever harm
You that trust the heavenly arm?
Dwelling in "the secret place,"
Presence of the God of grace.

What can harm thee—bid thee fear?
Ever sheltered—ever near.
Shadowed by the lasting rock,
Which defends—protects the flock.

He will guard thy life, thy breath;
Shield thee from the shafts of death,
When in terror's dark array;
Dread destruction walks by day.

When the deadly damps, they fall,
Gath'ring round the fatal pall ;
When dire pestilence, her hand
Raises, with remorseless wand,

God will there defend thy head,
And a covert for thee spread ;
" Give his angels charge to keep "
All thy walks by day—thy sleep.

Jesus made thy soul his care ;
He hath broke the "fowler's snare ;"
" He hath set his love on thee,"
Thou shalt his salvation see.

## The Path of Life.

" Thou wilt show me the path of life."

My God, my all-sufficient guide,
  On thee my soul is staid ;
I ask no other arm beside,
  Naught but thy hand for shade.

Thou art the shadow of the Rock
  Here in this weary land ;
The tender shepherd of that flock
  That bless thy faithful hand.

I know thou'lt lead, wilt guide secure,
　Wilt show the holy way—
The path of life, so bright and pure,
　That leads to perfect day.

The heavenly way, O make it plain
　Before my wavering sight ;
And let not all my hopes be vain,
　But deign my name to write—

With all the truly sanctified
　Who walk with God below,
In that blest book thou didst provide
　For them—thy love who know.

Though here beset with fears, with sin,
　A dang'rous, thorny road,
Through Thee I shall the vict'ry win,
　Oh Christ, my Saviour, God.

## Unwavering Trust.

" Fear ye not, stand still and see the salvation of the Lord, which he will
show you to-day."

Distrust, in pall of anguish,
　Has wrapped the Hebrew host,
They meet the deep, deep waters,
　They've reached the verge—the coast.
The oppressor now is hasting—
　His chariots are near,

And hope no more the sadness
  Presumes to light—to cheer;
The apathetic mountains,
  A pass they now deny,
And faith, her drooping pinions
  Are found too weak to try!
Know, Israel, thy helper,
  God of the wave, the hill;
Fear not, but wait before him,
  In holy trust be still;
His arm shall bring salvation,
  You shall deliv'rance see;
The Lord, he hath descended,
  His hand hath made thee free.

---

### Unfailing Mercy.

"His mercy endureth forever."

Oh! bless the glorious giver,
He will forsake thee never,
His mercy endureth forever;
  Now bless and praise the Lord;
His wisdom is unbounded,
With care he hath surrounded,
Our faith, it is well founded,
  Secure upon his word.

In heaven he ever reigneth,
His mighty hand sustaineth,
And his power and truth remaineth;
    His favors, they are showers,
He is our rock, most sure,
Forever to endure,
The holy, just, and pure,
    This gracious God is ours.

His grace, it faileth never,
Of life the well—the river,
And strong for to deliver
    From every form of ill;
Oh, ever adore and trust him,
And never, no, never, distrust him,
But bring a grateful anthem,
    Come, seek and do his will.

He's mercy for every nation,
Of highest or lowest station,
He off'reth to all salvation,
    In Christ, the glorious way
That leads direct to heaven,
Where golden harps are given,
To all the new arriven,
    There in the realms of day.

Glory to God, the highest,
Who mercy ne'er denyeth,
But evermore supplieth
    The living, that pervade

The ocean, earth, and air,
And heavenly regions fair,
For with a father's care
    Provision he hath made.

The raven and the sparrow,
They fear not for to-morrow;
Come, every child of sorrow,
    You have a mighty friend;
Come, if thy lot be dreary,
If sick, or sad, or weary,
Come, and the Lord will cheer thee,
    Will mercy on thee send.

## Paths of Mercy and Truth.

"All the paths of the Lord are mercy and truth unto such as keep his commandments."

Mercy paves thy pilgrim pathway,
    Drawn by the paternal hand,
Trav'ler, ye that now revereth
    Heaven—its law—its high commands.

Truth, her lamp, it waneth never
    For thee;—if it seem to fade,
Know, thou erring, weak believer,
    From its light thy foot hath strayed.

Mercy, with her gracious chalice,
    Walketh, watcheth all the day;
Truth hath made her habitation
    Ever in the narrow way.

All without is fearful!—fearful!
Darkness, fatal, reigns to hide
Lurking snares of death and danger
Which the foe, he hath supplied.

---

## The Pilot is Jesus.

" Then he arose, and rebuked the winds, and the raging of the water, and they
ceased, and there was a calm."

Oh, fearful! the winds and the waves are at war,
The watchful their vigils still keep,
But blind unbelief the vision would mar,
And lull the lost sinner to sleep.

See mercy's bright beacon, with heaven-kindled ray,
Is lighted to guide and to cheer ;
There's anchorage ground in yon placid bay,
Where moorings are safe from all fear.

Death's dark, low'ring tempest, is gathering near,
Its surges you may not control,
Now the ship, the blest Gospel, it speaks the most clear,
Ho ! welcome this life-boat, sad soul.

Oh, sinner, poor sinner, that harbor is free,
Look forth to the eternal shore ;
You ne'er shall be stranded—a Pilot you'll see,
The life-boat, 'twill take you safe o'er.

'Twill bear thee aloft, though billows swell high,
　　And fill thee with fear and dismay;
They may threaten thy bark, and ascend to the sky,
　　But the life-boat—'tis safe—you're away.

The Pilot is Jesus, that walked on the wave;
　　Who spake, and the storm it was o'er;
He'll bring thee to port—he's mighty to save,
　　And your anchor shall drag nevermore.

## Faith.

"Now faith is the substance of things hoped for, and the evidence of things
not seen."

The things now hid from mortal ken,
　　Within the vail, on high,
Faith, with her vision, ever sheen,
　　Alluringly brings nigh;
Substantial as the gracious throne
　　Evinced divinely clear,
The proofs she ever deigns to bring
　　The child of God to cheer.

Of that eternal, blest abode,
　　Port of the perfect rest
Where all the ransomed of the Lord
　　Forever shall be blest;
Shall drink from that immortal fount,
　　Life's pure, unfailing spring;
Oh, faith divine, what rays of bliss
　　Illume thy hand—thy wing.

'Twas by thy sanctifying light
　Prophets and elders found
The paths of truth and righteousness
　On this low, barren ground;
Obedient to thy kindly voice,
　Their ever-watchful ear
Received the mandate of the word
　Proclaimed so timely near.

'Tis through the medium held by thee
　We know this world so bright,
Came at the call of sovereign power
　From dark, chaotic night;
The orbs that through the ether fields
　Roll their unwearied round,
The valid witness of their birth
　Alone by thee is found.

Framed by the word of God alone,
　Designed by heavenly skill,
Thou hast the mirror where we trace
　The signet of his will,
Embodied in that mandate loud,
　Immutable and clear—
Decree that said, "Let there be light,"
　That bade each star appear.

The heaven-accepted sacrifice,
　The off'ring that was brought,
Type of the sanctifying flood,
　By faith was fully fraught;

The excellence of that perfume
　That reached the highest throne,
With righteous Abel's orison—
　It was by faith alone.

God, by his own indwelling power,
　This testimony gave,
That faith can find, can bring the gift
　That claims the grace to save;
Wisdom, and everlasting love,
　Pleased with the nectarine,
Bestrewed this altar—early reared,
　With favors all divine.

Death, with his arrow pointed drawn,
　Abashed, retires to see,
The mantle holy Enoch wore—
　The garb bestowed by thee;
Faith, hand-maid of the heavenly king,
　Who kindly deigned to spread
The panoply of paradise
　To guard his waiting head.

A passport robe of righteousness,
　Helmet—impervious mail;
Dress of such resurrection hue
　As they beyond the vale
Of pain, and sin, and care, and grief,
　In bliss, forever wear;
'Twas thine his walk with God to see,
　Thou led'st him safely there.

Without thy all-sufficient aid,
    That road may not be found,
That upward path, the paved highway,
    Where life and peace abound;
Recipients of that rich reward—
    The crown of life—of heaven,
To thee, O Faith, great polar star,
    Their helm below had given.

Relying on the Saviour's word,
    Thy children, heirs of rest,
Whose glorious inheritance
    Is found a portion blest;
Attracted by the shining coast,
    They launch the fearless bark,
With thee o'er rough and angry seas,
    Braved threat'ning billows dark.

We see thy architectural skill
    High on the deluge flood,
That merged a sin-polluted world—
    Long suffered;—warned of God;
Heir of thy own wrought righteousness,
    He saw the fabric rise,
Where unbelief profaned the Lord,
    His threat'nings dared despise.

Moved by the hand of filial fear
    He builded; watchful long;
A refuge from the verging storm,
    That whelmed the scoffing throng;

Faith, mighty helper of the past,
   Supporter of the low,
The fruit of every precious growth,
   'Tis thine to nurse, to sow.

When Abraham, servant of the Lord,
   The ancient call received,
'Twas by thy consecrating charm
   The promise he believed;
A stranger, pilgrim; heavenward bound,
   To thee a willing hand,
Gave—and thou leadest all the way,
   And cheered in distant land.

## The Prodigal.

### "I will arise, and go to my father."

I'll leave this land of want and care,
   I will arise, and go;
I'm perishing with hunger here,
   Where none will pity show;
This land, the witness of my sin,
   My servitude and shame;
My Father's pardon I would win,
   I'll own my guilt and blame;
Just as I am, I'll seek his face—
   He 's bread, and that to spare;
I'll only ask a servant's place,
   May I but shelter share;

I'll tell him how this spirit writhed
Beneath the frown of heaven,
Its anguish when the cup received,
In righteous judgment given.

The tender, fond, paternal eye,
That watched his coming long,
It doth the contrite one descry,
Forgets, forgives his wrong;
Compassion, tenderness and love,
The Father's heart divide,
He meets no more the haughty brow
That once his hand defied,
But floods of true, repentant tears,
From heart subdued, sincere,
Repay the Father's injured breast—
The lost is doubly dear;
His tattered garments, worn and soiled,
The choicest robes misplace,
And hands that sought the humblest toil,
Most costly rings they grace.

Now mirth and music rich abound,
With haste the feast is spread;
For this, the long-lost son is found,
Alive, as from the dead.

So, when a sinner turns to God,
With angels there is joy,
And all in the divine abode
Their golden harps employ.

## Heavenly Wisdom.

**" Wisdom is better than rubies."**

Above all price of rubic mine,
The pearls of heavenly wisdom shine ;
Oh, who their beauties ere would dare
To prize—with aught of earth compare ;
Her voice is heard throughout the waste
In words most excellent and chaste,
She loves to call, to win the youth,
Her lamp will guide in paths of truth.

Now, list to her, she will impart,
A wise and understanding heart,
Her lips, they drop with prudence sweet,
Where light and grace together meet ;
Her dwelling-place is hung around
With flowers of knowledge, heavenly ground.

She beck'neth to her glorious shrine,
All radiant with a light divine,
A counsellor forever near
When fainting hope would yield to fear ;
A shelter from the woes and strife
That strew the cloudy path of life.

By her the righteous scepter'd hand,
The kingly crown may bless the land,
And princes, too, inspired may wave,
By strength of wisdom, scepters brave ;

Her love is overflowing, free,
A well of life it sure shall be,
And they that early seek shall find
Its sacred waters well refined.

Riches and honors, they abound,
Where'er her gentle steps are found,
Riches most durable and rare,
Of righteousness divinely fair;
Her fruit with gold she'll not compare,
Her revenue we all may share,
The choicest silver—diamonds bright
But fade before her brilliant light;
She leads the way—this perfect guide,
She'll see thy treasures well supplied.

Then yield to her thy heart, thy love,
Her ark will bear thee safe above
To heaven, her throne, where high she dwelt,
And angels at her foot-stool knelt,
Before Jehovah's mighty hand
Had set to earth such beauties bland,

And spread the fountains of the deep
Where hidden diamonds silent sleep;
She held her counsels far on high,
Away beyond the ethereal sky;
When God, with infinite display
From chaos called and blest the day,

And strewed the azure vault, so clear,
With sparkling orbs, to grace, to cheer ;
With God, the ever-living God,
Wisdom the holy pavements trod,
Ever rejoicing in his sight,
Wisdom is truly " God's delight."

Oh, harken to her lovely voice,
Make her thy early, happy choice ;
You, in the blushing morn of days,
For blest are they that keep her ways.
The wisdom of God's ways and word,
Wisdom of Christ, our risen Lord,
But if we scorn and hate the right,
We love the road to deathless night.

---

## Charity Exemplified.

"Blessed is he that considereth the poor ; the Lord will deliver him in
time of trouble."

### LADY.

Oh, frown not on the beggar girl,
　　Haste not to close the door,
You may not know the anguish
　　That wrings that bosom's core ;
She may, in grief and sadness,
　　Now feel the orphan's woe,
Or weep, her faithful loved ones
　　By sickness now laid low.

Go, quickly, haste, and call her,
　　Go ask her to come in ;
To treat the poor so rudely
　　'Tis fearful, deadly sin !
'Tis late, and cold, and dreary,
　　And falling fast the snow,
Oh, mercy, pity, charity,
　　How could you tell her, no ?

Come in, poor little stranger,
　　Come, sit here by the fire ;
You're wet, and cold, and weary ?
　　Permit me to inquire—
I am your friend ; come, tell me,
　　Why you must ask for bread ?
I fear those tears that blind you
　　Are by an orphan shed ?

CHILD.

I am, my dear, kind lady,
　　Half-orphan—as they say,
And I feared my only parent,
　　She would have died to-day :
He's ill, my eldest brother,
　　And I must hasten home,
I left the children hungry—
　　They'll watch to see me come.

LADY.

Just stop a moment, daughter,
　　We'll send our man with you ;
He'll help you with your basket,
　　And take another, too.

Oh, Father of the Fatherless,
  Though joyful to receive,
It is thy promised blessedness
  When we thy poor relieve.

---

## A Flower Unique.

### TO A SISTER.

"For if we believe that Jesus died and rose again, even so them also that sleep
in Jesus will God bring with him."

Dear sister, take this flower,
  It grew on hallowed ground;
With trembling hand I plucked it
  From off that sacred mound;
The grave, where late our mother,
  We laid with hope so rife;
In Him, the resurrection—
  Who said—"I am the life."

A little vine, with tendrils,
  Had wound it round and round;
Half hidden by the branches,
  This lovely flower I found;
No hand, I knew, had planted it,
  No tear had there bedewed:
It grew so wild and lonely
  In that deep solitude.

I thought, perhaps, to class it—
  To find for it a name;
That Flora might interpret,
  Or tell from whence it came;

But vain were my researches,
This modest flower, so meek!
'Tis filial love shall name it—
We'll call it *Flower Unique.*

I know, with me, you'll cherish it,
It was the first to bloom;
The first to hold sad vigil
By our loved mother's tomb;
To cast its fragrant tribute
Above our honored dead,
To cheer the desolation
Where many tears were shed.

Though nameless, 't has a language—
It speaks with wondrous power;
Though silent, soft, and voiceless,
The language of a flower.
It has, indeed, a diction,
The eye of faith may read;
It adds a line—a precept,
Such as we ever need.

It tells us 'twas Infinity,
That planted there the vine;
'Twas God who taught the tendrils
Around the sod to twine;
That He who called the flowret,
From earth, so pure and fair,
Will not forget his covenant—
He knows the sleeper there.

# CONTENTS.

www.ingramcontent.com/pod-product-compliance
Lightning Source LLC
Chambersburg PA
CBHW020239090426
42735CB00010B/1760